# Look and Play
# Tractors

by Jim Pipe

Aladdin/Watts
London • Sydney

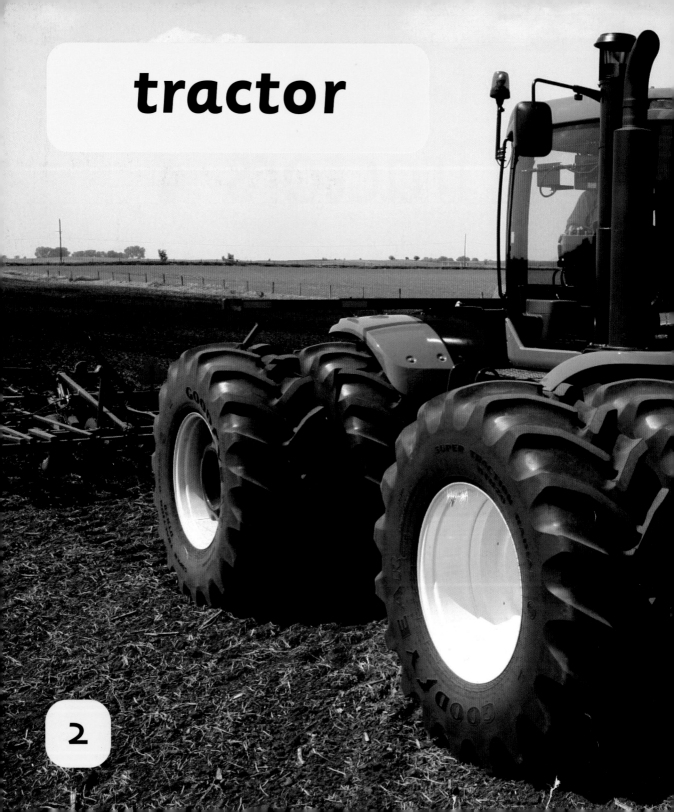

**tractor**

2

What does a **tractor** do?

3

**pull**

4

A tractor **pulls**.

5

**push**

6

A tractor **pushes**.

**plant**

A tractor **plants** seeds.

9

**plough**

10

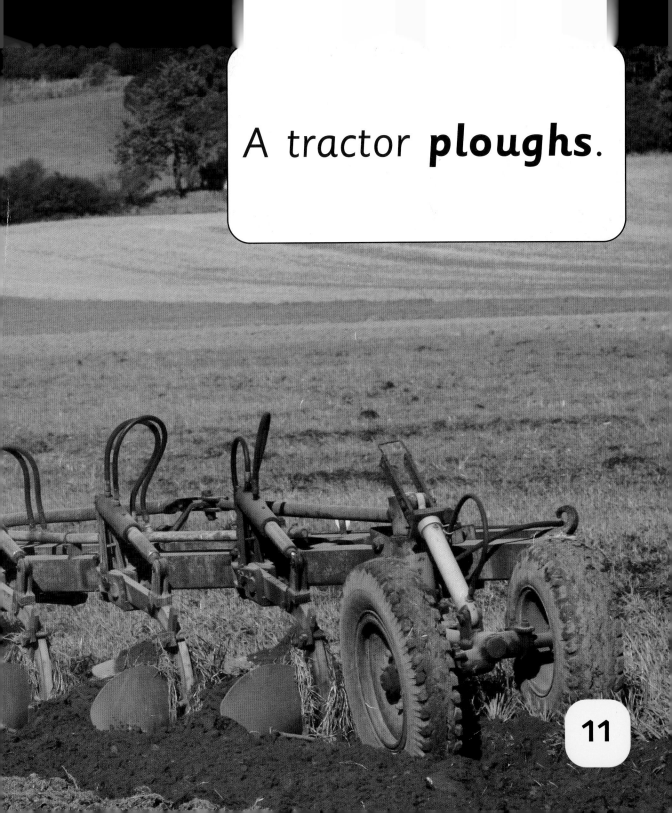

A tractor **ploughs**.

11

**spray**

A tractor **sprays**.

13

**mow**

A tractor **mows**.

15

**lift**

16

A tractor **lifts**.

17

**clear**

18

This tractor **clears** snow.

# What am I?

driver

engine

wheel

plough

Match the words and pictures.

# How many?

Can you count the tractors?

21

# What job?

What are these tractors doing?

# Index

23

# For Parents and Teachers

## Questions you could ask:

*p. 2 How many wheels does this tractor have?* Eight, though most tractors have four wheels. You could point out the large tyres, which help the tractor grip the ground when it is muddy/slippy.

*p. 6 Where does the driver sit?* In the cab, which is high up so the driver can see all around. The tractor here is piling up silage, grassy plants stored for cattle to eat during the winter.

*p. 8 Where do you think the seeds are stored?* The seeds are in the yellow buckets which this machine, known as a seed drill, drops onto the ground.

*p. 10 Can you see the plough? What do you think it does?* As a tractor pulls a plough, it digs long grooves in the soil called furrows that a farmer uses to plant (sow) seeds.

*p. 12 Can you see the clouds of spray?* The tractor sprays the crops with chemicals to stop weeds from growing and to stop insects from eating the crops.

*p. 14 Where have you seen a mower?* Mowing means cutting grass, e.g. lawnmower. When the grass is cut it dries out and is known as hay.

*p. 16 What is this tractor lifting?* The tractor is lifting a hay bale, which is used to feed animals such as cattle and sheep during the winter.

*p. 18 How does the tractor clear the snow?* It pushes it out of the way like a bulldozer then sprays the snow away from the road.

## Activities you could do:

• Organise a visit to a farm and watch a tractor at work, e.g. ploughing. Give each child a printed checklist to tick off the things they might see on the farm, e.g. animals, buildings, machines.

• Plan a day when children bring toy tractors into school. Ask them to describe all the different jobs the tractor can do, e.g. pushing, pulling, lifting and tipping loads, ploughing, planting seeds, mowing.

• Decorate a farm mural on a large piece of paper. Children can draw farm animals, tractors, barns etc.

• Introduce farms through songs such as "Old Macdonald" or "Baa Baa Black Sheep".

© Aladdin Books Ltd 2008

**Designed and produced by**
Aladdin Books Ltd
PO Box 53987
London SW15 2SF

**First published in 2008**
by Franklin Watts
338 Euston Road
London NW1 3BH

Franklin Watts Australia
Level 17/207 Kent Street
Sydney, NSW 2000

All rights reserved
Printed in Malaysia

A catalogue record for this book is available from the British Library.

Dewey Classification: 629.225'2

ISBN 978 0 7496 8624 6

Franklin Watts is a division of Hachette Children's Books, an Hachette Livre UK company.
www.hachettelivre.co.uk

**Series consultant**
Zoe Stillwell is an experienced Early Years teacher currently teaching at Pewley Down Infant School, Guildford.

**Photocredits:**
l-left, r-right, b-bottom, t-top, c-centre, m-middle.
All photos istockphoto.com except: 2-3, 14-15, 16-17, 20br, 22tl & br, 23tml, ml & br — courtesy New Holland. 8-9, 12-13 , 18-19, 21, 22bl, 23tl, bml & bmr – courtesy John Deere.